Financial Crimes Enforcement Network

Annual Report
Fiscal Year 2006

The Financial Crimes Enforcement Network (FinCEN) seeks to enhance U.S. national security and to make the financial system increasingly resistant to abuse by money launderers, terrorists and their financial supporters, and other perpetrators of crime. In pursuit of these aims, FinCEN relies on the expertise of a small but growing staff—now just over 300 employees—as well as on a broad range of collaborative partnerships.

As the nation's financial intelligence unit, FinCEN works closely with numerous federal, state, and local law enforcement agencies and regulators, as well as with members of our nation's diverse financial sectors. We also play a global leadership role in the Egmont Group of financial intelligence units, collaborate with our counterparts in other countries, and support multi-national bodies seeking to promote global anti-money laundering and counter-terrorist financing measures.

FinCEN's Fiscal Year 2006 accomplishments are a testament to both our employees' expertise and our many productive relationships with other agencies. This year, the men and women of FinCEN:

- Worked hand-in-hand with authorized users of Bank Secrecy Act (BSA) data to facilitate greater exploitation of this valuable financial information. For example, we expanded the capacity to broaden the scope of BSA data analysis through new sharing arrangements with several federal law enforcement agencies that use this data in combination with other unique data sets. We also provided all users who access BSA data via FinCEN's secure web an upgraded query system developed by the Internal Revenue Service, an accomplishment that required close coordination with a multitude of organizations.

- Supported law enforcement efforts through more than one thousand information exchanges with other members of the Egmont Group of financial intelligence units from around the world.

- Found innovative ways to analyze the BSA data to support industry, regulatory, and law enforcement needs. For example, at the request of law enforcement agencies, we developed major threat assessments based on financial activity in states along the U.S. southwest border and analyzed financial crime trends, patterns, and vulnerabilities in other geographic regions. We also examined trends in SAR filings, found particular industry sectors that may be vulnerable to illicit activity, and shared that information with our partners.

- Continued to enhance the effectiveness and uniformity of BSA compliance activity by developing additional information exchange agreements with federal and state supervisory agencies and updated the interagency Bank Secrecy Act/Anti-Money Laundering Examination Manual, which is designed to ensure consistent BSA application and compliance.

- Consulted with many stakeholders to develop regulations extending BSA suspicious activity reporting and anti-money laundering requirements to the insurance industry and extending suspicious activity reporting requirements to mutual funds.

- Worked with other agencies and offices within the Treasury Department to issue final rules against two foreign banks designated as being of "primary money laundering concern" and to issue a final regulation requiring certain U.S. financial institutions to engage in appropriate, specific due diligence in connection with correspondent banking accounts maintained for certain foreign financial institutions. These actions, authorized by the USA PATRIOT Act, are expected to have global impact.

- Achieved an increase in the electronic filing of BSA reports by providing financial institutions with outreach and technical assistance. E-filing reduces costs and time needed for filing and improves the quality of reported data.

- Cooperated with federal regulators in a variety of financial sectors to take joint enforcement actions in cases of egregious violations of the Bank Secrecy Act.

Among the many individuals who led these accomplishments were former FinCEN Directors Robert W. Werner and William J. Fox. We thank both for their leadership during the year and view the achievements of Fiscal Year 2006 as a strong foundation for meeting our goals in the year ahead.

William F. Baity

William F. Baity
Acting Director, January 2007

Contents

The Financial Crimes Enforcement Network (FinCEN), a bureau within the U.S. Department of the Treasury's Office of Terrorism and Financial Intelligence, is our nation's financial intelligence unit. Financial intelligence units are national centers set up to collect financial information pursuant to a given nation's anti-money laundering/counter terrorist financing regime. Financial intelligence units analyze that data and make the data available to appropriate authorities for use in combating financial crime.

Our mission is to safeguard the financial system from the abuses of terrorist financing, money laundering, and other financial crime. A central way that we fulfill this responsibility is through our role as administrator of the Bank Secrecy Act, as amended. Among a broad range of interrelated activities, we:

- Issue, interpret, and support and enforce compliance with regulations implementing the Bank Secrecy Act, as amended by Title III of the USA PATRIOT Act of 2001;

- Support and coordinate compliance examination functions delegated to other federal regulators;

- Manage the collection, processing, storage, and dissemination of BSA data;

- Maintain a government-wide access service to the BSA data and network users with overlapping interests; and

- Conduct analysis in support of policy makers; law enforcement, regulatory, and intelligence agencies; and the financial industry.

Because illicit financial activity is not confined to our borders, we also work to build global cooperation, strengthen other countries' efforts to deter and detect financial crime, and promote international information sharing about financial crime. To meet these aims, we coordinate with and collaborate on anti-terrorism and anti-money laundering initiatives with our financial intelligence unit counterparts around the world.

To learn more about the Financial Crimes Enforcement Network, visit our website at www.fincen.gov.

The U.S. Department of the Treasury established the Financial Crimes Enforcement Network in 1990. Our initial charge was to establish a government-wide multi-source financial intelligence and analysis network. Our operations were expanded in 1994 to include regulatory responsibilities for administering the Bank Secrecy Act, one of the nation's most potent weapons for preventing abuse of the U.S. financial system by financial criminals and terrorist financiers.

The Bank Secrecy Act, enacted in 1970, authorizes the Secretary of the Treasury to issue regulations requiring that financial institutions keep records and file reports on certain financial transactions determined to have a high degree of usefulness in criminal, tax, regulatory investigations and proceedings, and certain intelligence and counter-terrorism matters. The authority of the Secretary to administer Title II of the Bank Secrecy Act (codified at 31 U.S.C. 5311-5330 with implementing regulations at 31 C.F.R. Part 103) has been delegated to the Director of the Financial Crimes Enforcement Network.

Under the Bank Secrecy Act, record keeping and reporting requirements cover a variety of financial industry sectors. These include—but are not limited to—depository institutions (e.g., banks, credit unions, and thrifts); brokers or dealers in securities; mutual funds; futures commission merchants and introducing brokers in commodities; money services businesses (e.g., money transmitters; issuers, sellers, and redeemers of money orders, travelers' checks, and stored value; currency dealers and exchangers; check cashers; and the U.S. Postal Service); casinos and card clubs, and dealers in precious metals, stones, or jewels.

The USA PATRIOT Act of 2001 amended and broadened the scope of the Bank Secrecy Act to focus on terrorist financing, as well as money laundering. The USA PATRIOT Act also gave FinCEN additional responsibilities and authorities in both important areas, and established the organization as a bureau within the Department of the Treasury.

In 2002, FinCEN became a bureau within the U.S. Department of the Treasury. In 2004, it became part of Treasury's new Office of Terrorism and Financial Intelligence. This is the lead office within the Department for fighting the financial war on terror, combating financial crime, and enforcing economic sanctions against rogue nations.

The Bank Secrecy Act (BSA) is the nation's first and most comprehensive federal anti-money laundering/counter-terrorist financing statute. Since it was enacted in 1970, the Bank Secrecy Act has been amended several times, most recently by the USA PATRIOT Act of 2001. In summary, the Bank Secrecy Act authorizes the Secretary of the Treasury to issue regulations requiring banks and other financial institutions to take a number of precautions against financial crime, including filing reports that have been determined to have a high degree of usefulness in criminal, tax, regulatory investigations and proceedings, and certain intelligence and counter-terrorism matters.

Additionally, the BSA's anti-money laundering program requirement helps financial institutions protect themselves, and thus the U.S. financial system, from abuse by financial criminals, and helps those institutions identify and mitigate the risks inherent in their operations. The BSA's record keeping and reporting requirements also increase transparency in the financial system and help to create a financial trail that law enforcement and intelligence agencies can use to track criminals, their activities, and their assets.

Twelve separate reports are required under the Bank Secrecy Act. The reports that are filed most often are:

- Currency Transaction Reports (CTRs), which are filed in connection with cash deposits, withdrawals, exchanges of currency, or other payments or transfers by, through, or to a financial institution involving a transaction (or multiple transactions by or on behalf of the same person) in currency exceeding $10,000. Currency transaction reporting requirements are a key impediment to criminal attempts to legitimize the proceeds of crime.

- Suspicious Activity Reports (SARs), which are filed in connection with transactions that financial institutions know, suspect, or have reason to believe may be related to illicit activity. These reports are especially valuable to law enforcement and intelligence agencies because they reflect activity considered problematic or unusual by financial institutions, casinos, money services businesses, and the securities industry. SARs contain sensitive information and, consequently, may be disclosed and disseminated only under strict guidelines. Unauthorized disclosure of SARs is a violation of criminal law.

Bank Secrecy Act Reports

◆ Currency Transaction Report (CTR)

◆ Currency Transaction Report by Casinos (CTR-C)

◆ Currency Transaction Report by Casinos - Nevada

◆ Designation of Exempt Person

◆ Report of Foreign Bank and Financial Accounts (FBAR)

◆ Report of International Transportation of Currency or Monetary Instruments (CMIR - Collected by U.S. Customs and Border Protection)

◆ Report of Cash Payments over $10,000 Received in a Trade or Business (8300)

◆ Suspicious Activity Report (SAR)

◆ Suspicious Activity Report by a Money Services Business (SAR-MSB)

◆ Suspicious Activity Report by Casinos and Card Clubs (SAR-C)

◆ Suspicious Activity Report by Securities and Futures Industries (SAR-SF)

◆ Registration of Money Services Business

The latest versions of these forms are available at www.fincen.gov.

Based on preliminary data from the Internal Revenue Service's Enterprise Computing Center - Detroit, which receives and processes BSA reports through a partnership with FinCEN, the number of BSA reports filed in Fiscal Year 2006 rose to approximately 17.6 million, compared to about 15.6 million in Fiscal Year 2005. Increases in the number of SARs and CTRs accounted for most of the rise. More than one million SARs were filed during the year.

The following chart shows preliminary Fiscal Year 2006 reporting figures for each type of BSA report.

Bank Secrecy Act Filings by Type, Fiscal Year 2006[1]

Type of Form	Filed in FY 2006
Currency Transaction Report (all types)	15,994,484
Suspicious Activity Report (for all covered industries)	1,049,149
Report of Foreign Bank and Financial Accounts	287,356
Registration of Money Services Business	19,937
Designation of Exempt Person[2]	84,613
Report of Cash Payments Over $10,000 Received in a Trade or Business (Form 8300)	162,309
Total[3]	**17, 597,848**

[1]   Figures were provided by the Internal Revenue Service Enterprise Computing Center - Detroit in October 2006.

[2]   The Designation of Exempt Person form enables depository institutions (banks, savings associations, thrift institutions, and credit unions) to use Currency Transaction Report exemption rules to eliminate the reporting obligation for transactions by business customers with routine needs for currency.

[3]   In addition, the U.S. Customs and Border Protection, U.S. Department of Homeland Security, reported that approximately 146,980 Reports of International Transportation of Currency or Monetary Instruments were filed in FY 2006. These paper reports are not included in the total or in e-filing calculations.

FinCEN encourages electronic filing of BSA reports to accelerate the secure flow of information from financial institution filers to law enforcement and regulatory agencies. In Fiscal Year 2006, about 45 percent of BSA reports were e-filed, compared with about 24 percent e-filed in Fiscal Year 2005. (The percentage e-filed in the last two months of the year is one of FinCEN's performance measures. During the last two months of Fiscal Year 2006, 48 percent of the reports were e-filed, compared with 29 percent during the last two months of Fiscal Year 2005.)

Testimony on Value of Bank Secrecy Act Data

"...the FBI enjoys a cooperative and productive relationship with FinCEN, the broker of BSA [Bank Secrecy Act] information. FBI cooperation with FinCEN has broadened our access to BSA information which, in turn, has allowed us to analyze this data in ways not previously possible.

"When BSA data is combined with the sum of information collected by the law enforcement and the intelligence communities, investigators are better able to 'connect the dots' and, thus, are better able to identify the means employed to transfer currency or move value. The result of this collaborative relationship and access to financial intelligence is a significant improvement in the efficiency of our investigation of terrorist financing matters."

"Abundant examples exist of activities noted in BSA [Bank Secrecy Act] reports which have added value to counterterrorism investigations, oftentimes in ways that could not have been predicted from the reports alone. BSA data allows for a more complete identification of the respective subjects such as personal information, non-terrorism related criminal activity, previously unknown businesses and personal associations, travel patterns, communication methods, resource procurement, and Internet service providers.

The value of BSA data to our anti-money laundering and counterterrorism efforts cannot be overstated..."

Michael F.A. Morehart, Section Chief, Terrorist Financing Operations Section,
Counterterrorism Division, Federal Bureau of Investigation
In testimony before the U.S. House of Representatives Committee on Financial Services,
Subcommittee on Financial Institutions and Consumer Credit
May 18, 2006

The Financial Crimes Enforcement Network's Strategic Plan for Fiscal Years 2006-2008 outlines four strategic goals plus a management goal:

Goal 1: Protect the financial system through effective administration of the Bank Secrecy Act.

Goal 2: Combat terrorism, money laundering, and other financial crime through analysis of BSA data and other relevant information.

Goal 3: Intensify international anti-money laundering collaboration through the global network of financial intelligence units.

Goal 4: Facilitate regulatory compliance, data management, and information through E-government.

Management Goal: Develop a more nimble and responsive management structure.

These goals reflect our role as a regulatory agency, our responsibilities for combating money laundering and terrorist financing, and our long-range vision for providing law enforcement and regulatory agencies with better access to the BSA data while supporting these agencies with more sophisticated and unique analyses. The Strategic Plan is available at www.fincen.gov.

This report lists major FinCEN accomplishments for each of these goals in Fiscal Year 2006 and describes our priorities for Fiscal Year 2007.

Major Accomplishments in Fiscal Year 2006

Bank Secrecy Act Compliance Activity

This year, we continued to make progress toward assuring the effectiveness and uniformity of BSA compliance activity in all covered industry sectors. We:

■ Negotiated seven new information exchange agreements with federal and state supervisory agencies that examine for compliance with the Bank Secrecy Act or similar state regulations. This brings the total of such agreements to 48, providing a nearly nationwide view of examination processes and findings.

■ Revised the interagency Bank Secrecy Act/Anti-Money Laundering Examination Manual developed last year in collaboration with the five federal banking agencies and the Office of Foreign Assets Control. The Examination Manual is designed to ensure consistent BSA application and compliance at all federally regulated banking organizations, including commercial banks, savings associations, and credit unions. The Examination Manual was modified to further clarify supervisory expectations and to incorporate regulatory updates since its initial release in June 2005. The revisions also draw upon feedback from the banking industry and examination staff.

■ Expanded our outreach programs to clarify BSA requirements for regulated industries. For example, we participated as speakers or panelists in 148 domestic and overseas outreach events, compared with 73 events in Fiscal Year 2005.

■ Strengthened our internal operations by implementing, refining, and incorporating into our standard operating procedures a case management system to track, monitor, and report the status of outstanding compliance matters.

■ Processed 241 cases involving financial institutions with significant BSA violations or deficiencies that were referred to FinCEN pursuant to various federal and state information-sharing agreements.

■ Referred 104 matters involving financial institutions with possible BSA deficiencies to other agencies with examination authority.

■ Issued two advisories to partner regulatory agencies relating to common BSA violations or deficiencies that we identified.

Bank Secrecy Act Regulatory Developments

We issued final BSA regulations requiring insurance companies to establish anti-money laundering programs and report suspicious activity. The final regulations apply to insurance companies that issue or underwrite certain specified "covered" products that present a significant risk of money laundering, terrorist financing, or other illicit activity. These covered products include permanent life insurance policies, other than group life insurance policies; annuity contracts, other than group annuity contracts; and other products with cash value or investment features. In connection with this reporting requirement, we developed a new SAR form (FinCEN Form 108) specifically for insurance companies.

We also extended BSA suspicious activity reporting requirements to mutual funds. As with the insurance company suspicious activity reporting requirement, this requirement is expected to provide highly useful information to law enforcement, tax, and regulatory agencies and mirrors reporting requirements already established for other financial institutions, such as banks, broker-dealers in securities, casinos, and money services businesses. Mutual funds were already subject to regulations requiring

the development, implementation, and maintenance of anti-money laundering programs and customer identification programs.

To reduce potential abuse of international correspondent banking relationships providing access to the U.S. financial system, we issued a final regulation implementing the general due diligence requirements of the foreign correspondent banking provisions and the general due diligence and enhanced scrutiny requirements of the private banking provisions of section 312 of the USA PATRIOT Act. The foreign correspondent banking regulation, which is expected to have an impact on global banking practices, requires certain U.S. financial institutions to engage in appropriate, specific due diligence in connection with correspondent banking accounts maintained for certain foreign financial institutions.

We also issued guidance regarding how the final regulation applies to mutual funds where shares are purchased or redeemed by a U.S. financial institution through the Fund/SERV system of the National Securities Clearing Corporation on behalf of a foreign financial institution, as well as to securities broker-dealers and futures commission merchants engaged in certain intermediated relationships.

Guidance and Advisories

During the year, we issued 21 significant pieces of BSA guidance, including:

- Guidance, issued jointly with the Commodity Futures Trading Commission, on Customer Identification Programs for futures commission merchants and introducing brokers in commodities.

- Two guidance pieces, one issued jointly with the federal banking agencies and the other jointly with the Securities and Exchange Commission and the Commodity Futures Trading Commission, regarding the sharing of SARs with head offices, controlling companies, or parent entities. The guidance permits banks, securities broker-dealers, futures commission merchants, and introducing brokers in commodities to share SARs with both domestic and foreign parent entities, within the parameters indicated in the guidance.

- An advisory to financial institutions warning that the U.S. Department of the Treasury has concerns that the Democratic People's Republic of Korea, acting through government agencies and associated front companies, may be seeking financial services to support illicit activities.

- An advisory to financial institutions regarding a potential money laundering threat involving Belarusian government senior regime elements, acting individually or through government agencies or associated front companies, seeking to move misappropriated Belarusian state assets, as well as proceeds from illicit arms sales to or through the U.S. financial system.

- An advisory to U.S. financial institutions so that they may better guard against an increasingly prevalent money laundering threat involving the smuggling of bulk U.S. currency into Mexico. This advisory warns of the potential misuse of relationships with U.S. financial institutions by certain Mexican financial institutions, including Mexican casas de cambio.

- Two sets of Frequently Asked Questions to assist insurance companies to understand and comply with the regulations requiring them to establish anti-money laundering programs and report suspicious activity.

- Guidance related to regulations implementing section 312 of the USA PATRIOT Act.

Rules Proposed

We issued an Advance Notice of Proposed Rulemaking seeking comments from the public, and particularly the money services business and the banking industries, on the issue of money services businesses establishing and maintaining banking services.

We have also proposed amending the BSA regulations relating to currency transaction reporting by casinos. Specifically, we have proposed to exclude, as reportable transactions in currency, jackpots from slot machines and video lottery terminals. We have also proposed to exclude certain transactions between casinos and currency dealers or exchangers and between casinos and check cashers as reportable transactions in currency. Finally, we are proposing several other amendments that would update or clarify the examples of "cash in" and "cash out" listed in the currency transaction reporting regulation.

We jointly issued an Advance Notice of Proposed Rulemaking seeking comments on lowering or, possibly, eliminating the threshold (presently, $3,000 or more) related to the recordkeeping rule and travel rule requirements regarding collecting, retaining, and transmitting information on funds transfers and transmittals of funds.

Balancing Costs and Benefits of Regulatory Regime

"Ensuring that we strike the right balance between the cost and benefit of this regulatory regime is, in my view, one of FinCEN's central responsibilities. Accordingly, it is vital that we continue to examine how we can more effectively tailor this regime to minimize the costs borne by financial institutions while at the same time ensuring that the law enforcement, intelligence, and regulatory communities receive the information they need."

Robert W. Werner,
Director, Financial Crimes Enforcement Network
Before the Senate Banking Committee
September 12, 2006

Enforcement Activity

To encourage greater compliance with BSA requirements in a variety of financial sectors, we took significant enforcement actions this year in situations involving egregious violations of the Bank Secrecy Act. (See the box on the following page.) Our goal in taking these actions was not only to resolve compliance issues in the institutions affected, but also to encourage other institutions within specific sectors to improve their anti-money laundering and suspicious activity reporting programs.

To improve the efficiency our of enforcement actions, we adopted and implemented revised internal procedures for processing enforcement matters. Over the year, our dedicated staff met their target time frame for completing enforcement matters.

Civil Money Penalties Assessed in Fiscal Year 2006

Working closely with appropriate regulators, we jointly assessed civil money penalties against the following:

- Banco de Chile – New York and Banco de Chile – Miami, for failure to implement and maintain an adequate anti-money laundering program and failure to file SARs on numerous large dollar value transactions by, for or on behalf of, a prominent politically exposed person and a family member and associate of the prominent politically exposed person.

- ABN AMRO Bank, N.V., for failure to apply an adequate system of internal controls at its North American Regional Clearing Center, which operated as a clearing institution for funds transfers in U. S. dollars. ABN AMRO violated the requirement to establish and implement an adequate anti-money laundering program and the requirement to report suspicious transactions, including activity involving "shell companies" organized in the United States as originators or beneficiaries. Financial institutions in Russia and other former Republics of the Soviet Union with correspondent accounts at the North American Regional Clearing Center served as originating or beneficiary institutions. ABN AMRO consented to a civil money penalty in the amount of $30 million, the largest penalty that FinCEN has ever assessed against a financial institution.

- Oppenheimer & Company, a securities broker-dealer in New York City, for failure to implement an adequate anti-money laundering program. This failure, in turn, led to Oppenheimer's failure to report several million dollars in suspicious transactions. The civil money penalty was the first significant penalty by FinCEN against a securities firm.

- The Tonkawa Tribe of Oklahoma and Edward E. Street, of Tonkawa, Oklahoma, for failure to develop and implement an anti-money laundering program, failure to properly identify customers, failure to create and retain certain records, failure to report suspicious transactions and transactions in currency, and structuring currency transactions.

Edward E. Street, who directed and oversaw day-to-day operations of the casino, failed to apply any measurable efforts to implement policies, procedures or internal controls for BSA compliance. The Tonkawa Tribal Gaming Commission undertook no measures to ensure that the casino had adopted and implemented a reasonably-designed, written program for compliance with the Bank Secrecy Act. This enforcement action was the first by FinCEN against an individual and a tribe for violations under the provisions of the Bank Secrecy Act and its implementing regulations applicable to casinos.

- Metropolitan Bank & Trust Company, New York Branch, for failure to establish and implement an adequate anti-money laundering program to manage the risks of money laundering involving funds transfers, and failures to file SARs.

- BankAtlantic of Fort Lauderdale, Florida, for failure to establish and implement an adequate anti-money laundering program to manage the risks of money laundering involving funds transfers, and failures to file SARs.

- Frosty Food Mart, a money services business in Tampa, Florida, for failure to establish and implement an adequate anti-money laundering program, which resulted in failures to file CTRs.

- Liberty Bank of New York for failure to implement an adequate anti-money laundering program and violations of the requirement to report suspicious transactions. The bank's anti-money laundering program lacked adequate internal controls and procedures to respond to information sharing requests from law enforcement under section 314(a) of the USA PATRIOT Act.

- Deprez's Quality Jewelry and Loans, Inc., a money services business in Louisville, Kentucky, for failure to register in a timely manner with FinCEN, failure to establish and implement an effective anti-money laundering program, and evasion of currency transaction reporting requirements through structured transactions.

Note: Not all civil money penalties assessed were payable to FinCEN.

Section 311

To safeguard the domestic financial system from overseas illicit activity, section 311 of the USA PATRIOT Act authorizes the Secretary of the Treasury to find foreign jurisdictions, foreign financial institutions, classes of international transactions, and types of accounts to be of "primary money laundering concern" and to impose special measures to address those concerns. FinCEN conducts in-depth analyses, including interagency consultation, to support section 311 findings. In all section 311 activities, we work closely with other offices within the U.S. Department of the Treasury's Office of Terrorism and Financial Intelligence.

In Fiscal Year 2006, the U.S. Department of the Treasury issued final rules against two banks designated as being of "primary money laundering concern" in 2004. They are the Commercial Bank of Syria (CBS), along with its subsidiary, the Syrian Lebanese Commercial Bank, and VEF Banka of Latvia (and its subsidiary, Veiksmes lizings). U.S. financial institutions are prohibited from opening or maintaining correspondent accounts for, or on behalf of, these banks and are responsible for monitoring for indirect access by both banks to the U.S. financial system through "nested" (intermediary) accounts.

CBS is owned and controlled by the Syrian government, a U.S.-government designated state sponsor of terrorism since 1979. CBS has been used by terrorists to move funds and has acted as a conduit for the laundering of proceeds generated from the illicit sale of Iraqi oil. VEF, one of the smallest of Latvia's 23 banks, maintains correspondent accounts in countries worldwide. FinCEN determined that VEF was a banking resource for illicit shell companies in financial fraud rings and permitted ATM withdrawals in significant amounts, an essential component of the execution of large financial fraud schemes. Since then, VEF has revised its policies and procedures, closed approximately 600 questionable accounts, and changed its management. Despite these steps, however, we have continued concern about reported links between the bank's ownership and organized crime groups that are suspected of facilitating money laundering.

During the year, we also withdrew our finding of April 2005 that Multibanka, another Latvian bank, was of primary money laundering concern. FinCEN had previously found reasonable grounds for concluding that Multibanka, the oldest commercial bank in Latvia, was used by criminals to facilitate or promote money laundering. After that finding, Multibanka took a number of steps to address reported money

Section 311 (continued...)

laundering risks. These included: revising its policies, procedures and internal controls; reviewing the entire portfolio of its accounts; retaining an international accounting firm to assist with development and auditing of its anti-money laundering program; and hiring additional employees to assist with compliance.

In addition, Latvia has made important strides in strengthening its national anti-money laundering/counter-terrorist financing regime, including passing legislation to significantly tighten anti-money laundering controls and increase associated penalties. Latvia has also banned the establishment of shell banks, introduced criminal liability for providing false information to banks, clarified the authority of Latvian financial institutions to demand information on the source of funds, and allowed information sharing between financial institutions on suspicious activity.

Cross-Border Wire Transfers

The Intelligence Reform and Terrorism Prevention Act of 2004 directed the Secretary of the Treasury to prescribe regulations to require the reporting to FinCEN of certain cross-border electronic transmittals of funds to help detect and prevent the proceeds of financial crimes and terrorist financing from flowing across America's borders. In preparation for implementing the regulation and data collection system, the Act requires the U. S. Department of the Treasury to study the feasibility of such a program and report its conclusions to Congress.

During Fiscal Year 2006, FinCEN took steps to assure that the regulation, if implemented, would address the needs and concerns of a broad array of stakeholders. In March, we conducted a survey of financial services industry trade groups to seek information about the feasibility and impact of implementing such a requirement. The American Bankers Association, the Institute of International Bankers, the Credit Union National Association, the Independent Community Bankers of America, America's Community Bankers, and others provided us with responses on behalf of their membership.

FinCEN has engaged members of the financial services industry and the federal financial regulatory agencies through the BSA Advisory

Group (see page 57). We have also engaged separately with our partners in the law enforcement community through meetings with their representatives and through the distribution of surveys to those agencies to assess what value might be derived from such reporting in the context of their missions. Likewise, FinCEN had extensive discussions with the federal financial industry regulatory agencies, particularly the staff of the Board of Governors of the Federal Reserve System. The financial intelligence units in Canada and Australia, which already require financial institutions to report cross-border wire transfers, also provided extensive assistance.

FinCEN concludes that implementation of a regulation and the technological systems for collecting cross-border fund transfer data is feasible, and has identified potential value in collecting cross-border electronic wire transfer information. However, FinCEN concludes that it is unrealistic to complete such a system by December 2007, as the statute requires. FinCEN estimates the effort will require approximately three years.

During its study, FinCEN also identified a number of policy-related concerns that warrant further consideration. Chief among these is how to protect the privacy of individuals about whom we collect information. Another concern is the costs such a reporting requirement would impose on U.S. financial institutions. Last, there is some concern about the potential impact of the proposed reporting requirement on the day-to-day operations of electronic wire transfer systems in the United States.

In the study, FinCEN proposes an approach to resolving these policy issues that would provide the opportunity to alter or halt the effort before FinCEN or the U.S. financial services industry incurs significant costs. Over a period of nearly one year, FinCEN would: (1) develop detailed user requirements to meet the needs of those who access BSA data; (2) work with representatives of the U.S., Canadian, and Australian financial services industry, and the major payment systems, to quantify the costs of implementation and compliance; and (3) obtain and analyze a sample of cross-border wire transfer data, and explore means of extracting value from the data. Based on these efforts, FinCEN would create a development plan incorporating milestones and pilot testing for different aspects of the reporting system.

Value of Wire Transfer Data in Protecting Economic and National Security

"If we can identify data in cross-border wire transfer records that helps protect economic and national security and find a workable way to efficiently collect that data–all while protecting and preserving its integrity–it will enormously strengthen our efforts. At the same time, we need to ensure that we do not impose regulatory requirements on the industry without the promise of real anti-money laundering and anti-terrorist funding benefits."

Robert W. Werner, Director, Financial Crimes Enforcement Network
In a press release describing survey on feasibility and impact of implementing a
cross-border wire transfer reporting requirement
March 10, 2006

Financial Action Task Force Mutual Evaluation

In the international arena, FinCEN provided staff support and information for the third mutual evaluation of the U.S. overall anti-money and counter-terrorist financing regime by the Financial Action Task Force on Money Laundering (FATF). FATF is an inter-governmental organization established in 1989 to develop and promote national and international policies to combat money laundering and terrorist financing.

FATF requires member countries to undergo a periodic mutual evaluation based on a methodology linked to FATF's 40 Recommendations on Money Laundering and Nine Special Recommendations on Terrorist Financing. The 40+9 Recommendations provide a complete set of

aspirational counter-measures against money laundering and terrorist financing covering the criminal justice system and law enforcement, the financial system and its regulations, and international co-operation.

The U.S. was found to have significantly strengthened its overall anti-money laundering and counter-terrorist financing measures since its last mutual evaluation in June 1997, implementing a very large number of statutory amendments and structural changes. The most high-profile development was the enactment of the USA PATRIOT Act.

The evaluation also determined that U.S. authorities are committed to identifying, disrupting, and dismantling money laundering and terrorist financing networks. Additionally, it was noted that the U.S. has produced impressive results in terms of prosecutions, convictions, seizures, asset freezing, confiscation and regulatory enforcement actions. Although FATF expressed concerns about the extent to which U.S. financial institutions require information on beneficial ownership, the availability of corporate ownership information, and the lack of regulatory requirements for certain non-financial businesses and professions, the United States was applauded for its robust program. The complete report is available at **http://www.fatf-gafi.org/data-oecd/44/9/37101772.pdf**.

The evaluation process required more than 18 months of interagency collaboration, research, and writing, and four weeks of meetings with on-site visitors from an international team of FATF assessors. It further included a "face-to-face" meeting in Paris, France where assessment findings and ratings were negotiated. The final assessment report was adopted and made public at a FATF Plenary meeting in June.

FinCEN provided case analysis, legal support, statistics, and a thorough, detailed explanation of the BSA regulatory regime. Staff also represented FinCEN at the on-site meetings with the assessors, at the face-to-face negotiations in Paris, and at the June FATF Plenary.

Major Accomplishments in Fiscal Year 2006

During Fiscal Year 2006, FinCEN continued to support law enforcement, regulatory, and intelligence partners and foreign financial intelligence units in our mutual goals of combating terrorism, money laundering, other financial crimes and threats to national and global security. Of particular note were our efforts to increase the support to our customers through high-impact, specialized, and unique analyses of BSA data rather than straightforward database queries. In addition, we proactively identified individuals and networks associated with suspicious financial activity and referred that information to appropriate law enforcement agencies.

Domestic Geographic Threat Assessments

We developed a number of analytical products specifically tailored to our law enforcement customers' needs. These included:

■ Three major assessments of financial activity in states along the U.S. southwest border to support state and federal drug and cash interdiction efforts. These three assessments, based on analysis of all BSA reports filed in border counties, identified potential money laundering hotspots and significant changes in financial activity to help state and federal authorities allocate resources on the southwest border. FinCEN's clients for these assessments included the Texas Department of Public Safety, the Arizona Attorney General's Office, the El Paso Intelligence Center, the Office of National Drug Control Policy, and the National Drug Intelligence Center. The reports are for Official Use Only and are available to law enforcement, regulatory, and intelligence agencies.

■ Analyses of trends, patterns, and financial crime vulnerabilities in the states of Maryland and California, and the city of Youngstown, Ohio. All of these reports were requested by law enforcement agencies, included an analysis of SARs and other BSA reports filed in the target area and are for Official Use Only.

Industry Analyses

FinCEN analysts assessed financial crimes vulnerabilities in 11 industries or industry sectors. Studies covered the credit card and credit union industry; check cashing companies; unregistered money services businesses; digital currency; and several products offered in the insurance industry. Industry analyses also assessed evolving trends in illicit finance, including mortgage fraud and abuse of loadable stored value cards. Our internal regulatory analysts and external regulatory partners are using these analyses to evaluate regulatory needs and policies in the sectors assessed.

Analysts also completed an assessment of the vulnerability of the limited liability company (LLC) structure and formation process to abuse in illicit international financial transactions. This assessment, which analyzed BSA filings as well as LLC formation and reporting requirements, helped to form the basis for FinCEN's recommendations for increased regulation of state business incorporation practices. Using a secure web connection, FinCEN provided this assessment to regulators and law enforcement agencies, and it contributed to coordination among federal agencies investigating abuse of LLCs.

Financial Institution Reviews

FinCEN analysts provided support to our regulatory colleagues and partners through reviews of 68 unique financial institutions. Thirty-four of these financial institutions were referred to FinCEN by federal regulatory authorities with whom we have signed Memoranda of Understanding (MOU) containing information-sharing commitments. Analysts combined research and analysis of BSA reports, commercial and law enforcement database records, and open source information to produce comprehensive, detailed products used to determine the examined institutions' compliance with Bank Secrecy Act, USA PATRIOT Act, and anti-money laundering program requirements. Separate from the MOU process, analysts examined compliance-related matters at 14 other financial institutions and developed analytical products concerning another 20 institutions considered for enforcement action and civil money penalties.

Postal Money Order Guide

As part of our Technical Reference series, we published a comprehensive, Official Use Only guide for law enforcement agencies on the mechanisms used for postal service money orders. The guide provides investigative officials with information about the operation of the money order industry and its vulnerabilities related to use in money laundering. In addition to publishing the guide, FinCEN conducted in-depth training sessions to assist law enforcement agencies in investigating cases involving money orders.

Value of Bank Secrecy Act Information

During the year, FinCEN continued its programs to ensure that law enforcement agencies, regulatory partners, and the financial industries are aware of the value and uses of BSA data. FinCEN's regulatory analysts provided 27 presentations to industry members and associations, regulators, law enforcement representatives, and visiting foreign FIU dignitaries to explain the analytical use and value of BSA data and to demonstrate the analytical tools used at FinCEN.

In the law enforcement arena, we documented instances in which information from BSA reports was used to identify or build cases against individuals and networks who pleaded guilty to or were convicted of a wide variety of financial crimes, including money laundering, illegal transfer of funds to Iran, real estate fraud, embezzlement, illegal check cashing, drug trafficking, and insurance fraud. Cases were described in the *SAR Activity Review – Trends, Tips & Issues*, published on FinCEN's public web site, and posted to the secure system through which authorized law enforcement and regulatory users gain access to BSA data.

Increased Secure Information Sharing with Financial Institutions

FinCEN upgraded its 314(a) Secure Information Sharing System to increase security and implement a disaster recovery capability. This system enables federal law enforcement agencies, through FinCEN, to reach out to more than 48,000 points of contact at more than 27,000 U.S. financial institutions to locate accounts and transactions of persons that may be involved in terrorism or significant money laundering. FinCEN is also utilizing this system to provide more frequent information alerts to financial institutions.

Collaboration with Foreign Financial Intelligence Units

As the financial intelligence unit for the United States and one of the founding members of the Egmont Group, FinCEN has played a lead role in developing and expanding global information exchanges needed to combat money laundering and terrorist financing. Our analytical efforts and information exchanges are included in the next section of this report.

January 12, 2006
Excerpt from Treasury Press Release

U.S. Money Laundering Threat Assessment Released

The United States Government today released the inter-agency U.S. Money Laundering Threat Assessment (MLTA), the first government-wide analysis of its kind, which investigates money-laundering vulnerabilities across a spectrum of techniques used by criminals.

"Before you can effectively treat a problem, you must first have an accurate diagnosis. The Money Laundering Threat Assessment integrates information contributed by 16 government agencies, as well as vital BSA data provided to Treasury's Financial Crimes Enforcement Network (FinCEN) to evaluate the range of current and emerging U.S. money laundering threats," said Stuart Levey, Treasury's Under Secretary for Terrorism and Financial Intelligence (TFI). "This is an example of government cooperation at its best."

Sixteen U.S. bureaus, offices, and agencies from the U.S. Departments of Treasury, Justice, Homeland Security, the Board of Governors of the Federal Reserve System, and the United States Postal Service collaborated on the MLTA. The Financial Crimes Enforcement Network provided analysis for the publication.

Major Accomplishments in Fiscal Year 2006

Financial Intelligence Unit Development

During Fiscal Year 2006, the Financial Crimes Enforcement Network continued to play a leadership role in helping other countries develop and strengthen their financial intelligence units (FIUs). For example, we:

- Provided two week-long, hands-on analytical training sessions for the Nigerian FIU in Abuja, Nigeria. Class topics included Analytical Critical Thinking, Suspicious Transactions Report Analysis, Charting Techniques, Sources of Information, and the Analysis Cycle. Attendees included FIU and law enforcement personnel, prosecutors, and Central Bank personnel.

- Gave a presentation on FinCEN's outreach efforts at a seminar on money services businesses conducted in Jamaica for English-speaking Caribbean countries. We also helped the Jamaican FIU acquire funding from the U.S. Department of State, the U.S. Embassy, and the United Kingdom High Commission for urgently needed information technology hardware and software.

- Hosted delegations from the nascent FIU in India and from the Albanian FIU. Representatives were provided briefings about and demonstrations of FinCEN operations, the U.S. regulatory regime, analytical tools and processes, and briefings from outside regulatory and law enforcement agencies.

- Conducted an on-site visit jointly with the Bahamian and Canadian FIUs to the Dominican Republic to discuss Egmont membership criteria.

- Conducted other onsite assessments and visits in Malaysia for information technology technical assistance.

Assessments

FIUs seeking membership in the Egmont Group must first be assessed by member FIUs in order to ensure that the strength of their regulatory regimes and programs meet established criteria. (See page 58 for a description of the Egmont Group.) Additionally, FinCEN participates jointly with foreign and domestic organizations and agencies to conduct a number of other types of assessments, including technical assistance needs assessments, financial sector assessments, and Financial Action Task Force (FATF) and FATF-style regional body mutual evaluations of member states. During FY 2006, we:

- Joined with Canada's FIU, FINTRAC, to conduct a joint technical assistance needs assessment for Suriname, which the U.S. is sponsoring for Egmont Group admission.

- Conducted an onsite assessment of the FIU in Saudi Arabia, and shared our findings with Cypress and Lebanon, with whom we are co-sponsoring Saudi Arabia for Egmont Group membership.

- Conducted the law enforcement portion of the FATF mutual evaluation of Switzerland. We also drafted and defended the law enforcement section of that mutual evaluation report at the FATF Plenary in Paris, France.

We used our expertise in the international financial arena to write 110 country assessments on financial crimes, money laundering, and terrorist financing for the International Narcotics Control and Strategy Report published by the U.S. Department of State.

Collaboration with Other Financial Intelligence Units

We collaborated and communicated with many other FIUs and governments in Fiscal Year 2006 on efforts to strengthen counter-terrorist financing and anti-money laundering programs and policies world wide. For example, we:

- Worked with representatives from the FIUs of Argentina, Brazil, and Paraguay on an analysis of financial crimes in the Triborder Area (TBA) spanning those three countries. The TBA is a suspected locus of illicit activities, including terrorist financing, drug trafficking, bulk cash smuggling, and intellectual property rights violations. The project utilizes SAR data to identify suspicious trends, patterns, and money flows in the TBA. In addition to providing valuable information regarding suspected criminal activity, the project furthered ongoing multilateral efforts to combat money laundering and terrorist financing in the TBA.

- Along with Treasury's Office of Technical Assistance, we visited the Malaysian FIU to further information exchanges. We also participated in a financial investigations seminar in Romania.

- Coordinated development of a database containing FIU and law enforcement data concerning money laundering and terrorist financing cases. We worked with the FIUs in Belgium and Canada on this project, which is designed to facilitate identification of trends and typologies.

Information Exchanges

As part of our information-sharing with Egmont Group members, FinCEN responds to requests for research from other FIUs. These requests have increased every year for the last six years, reaching 792 in Fiscal Year 2006. The rise has been spurred by the growing number of FIUs, as well as by greater international information sharing to combat money laundering, terrorist financing, and other crimes. In Fiscal Year 2006, the Egmont Group had 101 members, almost a third of whom were admitted within the last four years. This dramatic growth in membership resulted in a corresponding 30 percent increase during 2004-2006 in the number of incoming requests that FinCEN receives from foreign FIUs.

As the U.S. financial intelligence unit, FinCEN serves as the nation's channel for domestic law enforcement agencies seeking information from other FIUs. We received 131 such requests from domestic law enforcement agencies in Fiscal Year 2006 and referred them to 80 different FIUs.

Money Laundering Scheme Transferred over $12 Million to South American Countries

Six people were convicted and sentenced for their involvement in a $12 million money laundering scheme. The scheme involved the wire transfers of drug proceeds to South American countries for the benefit of drug cartels.

The defendants deposited drug proceeds into more than 50 bank accounts in the name of front companies, and then transferred the funds to various countries. The defendants also wired nearly $1 million through money transmitting businesses in amounts under $10,000 in an attempt to avoid federal reporting requirements.

This case originated with the filing of a SAR and was investigated by Internal Revenue Service-Criminal Investigation.

(Source: Internal Revenue Service)
Reported in the October 2005 issue of the SAR Activity Review

International Working Groups and Conferences

Director Werner gave the keynote speech at the 10th Hemispheric Congress on Money Laundering and the Financing of Terrorism. Some 430 banking officials from 18 countries participated in the meeting, which was held in Panama. The Director called attention to the proliferation of shell companies that are used as fronts to launder money, and he emphasized the need for international cooperation and joint efforts among authorities and the private sector in the fight against this threat.

We also participated in other multilateral fora to discuss ways to strengthen anti-money laundering and counter terrorist financing programs and initiatives. FinCEN delegates participated in the Egmont Group Plenary and Working Group meetings, the Financial Action Task Force, the Caribbean Financial Action Task Force, the Eastern and Southern Africa Anti-Money Laundering Group, the Financial Action Task Force of South America, the Council of Europe Select Committee of Experts on the Evaluation of Anti-Money Laundering Measures (MONEYVAL), the Eurasian Group on Combating Money Laundering and Financing of Terrorism, the Asia Pacific Group, and the Middle East & North Africa Financial Action Task Force.

Egmont Secure Web

FinCEN developed and maintains the Egmont Secure Web to facilitate communications and information sharing among Egmont Group members. In Fiscal Year 2006, after receiving input from our partner FIUs through the Egmont Information Technology Working Group, we initiated significant upgrades to the Egmont Secure Web to increase reliability, upgrade security, and enhance communications between FIUs. We also connected five new financial intelligence units to the Egmont Secure Web and worked with the FIU in the Netherlands on a plan to integrate the Egmont Secure Web and FIU.NET, a network that enables FIUs from the European Union to share financial intelligence quickly and securely.

Key Global Activity, Fiscal Years 2004 - 2006

	FY 2004	FY 2005	FY 2006
Number of countries to which FinCEN provided assistance in establishing financial intelligence units	11	9	10
Number of multinational fora in which we participated	N/A	N/A	15
Number of financial intelligence units newly connected to Egmont Secure Web during fiscal year	20	9	5
Total number of financial intelligence units connected to Egmont Secure Web	84	93	98
Number of information requests to and from foreign jurisdictions to support law enforcement cases	N/A	1,022[1]	1,002[2]

[1] Total includes 645 closed cases from FIUs and 377 requests to FIUs.

[2] Total includes 680 closed cases from FIUs and 322 requests to FIUs.

Major Accomplishments in Fiscal Year 2006

Use of Bank Secrecy Act Data

The number of authorized users of BSA data grew significantly between the end of Fiscal Year 2005 and Fiscal Year 2006, as we expanded and improved our methods for providing that data to authorized law enforcement and regulatory agencies. For example, we expanded the dissemination of entire BSA data sets to federal law enforcement agencies for use with internal warehouse applications and database systems. Some 2,457 federal users were mining the data at the end of the fiscal year, compared with 1,154 a year earlier. A key user of the data is the Federal Bureau of Investigation (FBI), which has been designated the nation's lead agency for terrorist financing investigations. The FBI has incorporated BSA data into its Investigative Data Warehouse (IDW), which contains multiple sources of counterterrorism data.

In addition, 4,683 users had access to the BSA data through FinCEN's secure web-based system at the end of FY 2006, compared with less than 4,000 a year earlier.

E-Filing

We continued to provide outreach and technical assistance to promote electronic filing of BSA reports. Specifically, we identified the largest filers and developed an outreach plan for helping them move to e-filing. We also upgraded security processes for e-filing and devoted new staff to providing e-filing user support, including new user authentication, and password distribution.

Approximately 48 percent of BSA reports were electronically filed during the last two months of Fiscal Year 2006, up from 29 percent during the corresponding months in Fiscal Year 2005. Increased e-filing resulted in cost efficiency, as the cost per e-filed report dropped from $.32 in Fiscal Year 2005 to $.22 in Fiscal Year 2006.

Transition to New Web System for Accessing BSA Data

Using a rapid deployment plan, FinCEN provided all employees and external users who query BSA data via FinCEN's secure web system access to Web CBRS, a server-based system developed by the Internal Revenue Service (IRS). The IRS collects and houses the BSA data under a longstanding partnership with FinCEN. Web CBRS replaced the IRS Currency and Banking Retrieval System (CBRS), a mainframe-based system formerly required for data queries.

The new system has a more intuitive interface and expanded user functionality, including the ability to query a larger variety of data fields and to conduct narrative keyword searches on all SAR forms. It also provides greater flexibility for querying and downloading large datasets for further analysis.

In conjunction with deploying the new system, we enhanced our Help Desk and our capabilities for authorizing and connecting users more expeditiously. Help Desk personnel, processing specialists, and liaisons or agents now collaborate to set up user access, handle technical questions, and help users navigate the system and comprehend the BSA data. To maximize training opportunities for current and new users, we conducted regional training conferences around the country and simultaneously maintained an online training program. We also expanded our onsite inspection program, previously conducted for state and local law enforcement users, to federal law enforcement agencies, federal and state regulators, and other agencies.

Excerpts from FinCEN Press Release
July 13, 2006

FinCEN Halts BSA Direct Retrieval and Sharing Project

The Financial Crimes Enforcement Network (FinCEN) today announced it will permanently halt the current BSA Direct Retrieval and Sharing Component (BSA Direct R&S) project. The project has repeatedly missed program milestones and performance objectives and the current performance of the system does not meet the needs of FinCEN's users. The level of effort and costs to complete BSA Direct R&S, address all remaining defects of the system, and operate and maintain the system, are likely to be much greater than originally projected. Going forward, FinCEN will inventory its capacity, assess its needs and the needs of its customers, and begin planning for future capabilities for retrieval, sharing and enhanced analysis of the BSA data.

"I am disappointed that this part of the BSA Direct project, which was an ambitious one, could not be completely salvaged," said Robert W. Werner, Director of the FinCEN. "However, in good conscience, I could not devote further resources to the project when I can find no guarantee that any amount of added spending would ever produce the desired result. This decision is in the best interest of the government, of the taxpayers, and of our law enforcement customers."

FinCEN launched BSA Direct R&S, a data warehouse and information retrieval system, in July 2004 as a component of BSA Direct, an umbrella project with several components including retrieval and sharing, electronic filing, and secure access. The electronic filing and secure access components have been operational for a number of years. The development of BSA Direct R&S was aimed to improve authorized users' ability to analyze and access BSA data. It was intended to apply data warehousing technology to structure the data in a single, integrated, secure web-based environment, and provide more sophisticated business intelligence and other analytical tools in a user-friendly web portal.

FinCEN's law enforcement customers are not significantly impacted by the decision to halt BSA Direct R&S. They can continue to use FinCEN's Secure Outreach system to access BSA data, and soon will transition to the IRS' Web CBRS for retrieval and online analysis of BSA information.

Major Accomplishments in Fiscal Year 2006

Investment, Project, and Portfolio Management

To improve our internal management capabilities, we established more rigorous processes for governing information technology investment decisions and financial oversight. We also took the first steps toward setting up a Project Management Office that will improve project and project portfolio management. We hired an expert with the background needed to establish the office, and contracted with an external firm for related consulting services. The new office will aim to enhance project management skills across the bureau through education, mentoring, and use of proven project management methodologies. The office will also manage a portfolio of our key projects.

Infrastructure Assessment and Improvement

To identify ways that we could improve our information technology foundation, we arranged for two external consultants to evaluate and assess our technology infrastructure. A team from the National Security Agency conducted an assessment of our network vulnerability. Following the assessment, we took immediate action to strengthen items identified as needing attention. A second external consultant then assessed our infrastructure and recommended several improvements, which will be made next year.

Staff Hiring, Training, and Performance Management

We strengthened our total force from 291 to 299 employees during the year. To help both new and experienced staff develop their expertise, we provided 286 training opportunities for our employees, including technical or job skills training for 264 employees and management skills training for 97 percent of our managers. Training opportunities included external programs, as well as programs developed in-house to meet specific needs of a wide variety of FinCEN employees.

We also completed the first cycle of a bureau-wide, multi-tier performance management system for employees, which was introduced in Fiscal Year 2005. We developed a comprehensive awards policy to reward excellent performance, trained managers in key skills relating to conducting performance appraisals, and set up a management review process to ensure consistency of results across the bureau.

Leadership Development Planning

To prepare the next generation of FinCEN leaders, we developed a succession planning strategy. The plan includes programs for building needed skills, mentoring, and regular in-house professional development.

Financial Management

Prudent financial management is an ongoing bureau priority. As stewards of public resources, we ensured that management control systems provided reasonable assurance of compliance with the Federal Managers Financial Integrity Act.

Internal Communications

To improve communications and knowledge-sharing between employees in different FinCEN offices and divisions, we:

- Instituted a program of conducting quarterly "Town Hall" meetings that focus on news of interest to all employees, including progress toward meeting our performance measures and goals.

- Redesigned our employee Intranet to make it more informative, easier to use, and more dynamic.

- Published six issues of an employee newsletter reporting our progress toward meeting our strategic goals.

- Began a project to promote collaborative efforts across organizational lines.

Employee Programs

We promoted diversity awareness and wellness among employees by presenting four special emphasis programs addressing gender, ethnic, health issues and persons with disabilities in the workplace. We offered employees a time management seminar and four additional personal development sessions. We also presented five additional community-building and employee recognition programs, such as Diversity Day and Bring Your Child to Work Day.

Program Assessments

We conducted Program Assessment Rating Tool program evaluations for all bureau programs not previously assessed. These included our programs involving data analysis, liaison with law enforcement and financial intelligence unit partners, and regulatory activity. Results are described in the Program Evaluations section of this report.

F inCEN's priorities for the next fiscal year build on our accomplishments in Fiscal Year 2006 and respond to the continuing threats and challenges of both domestic and international financial crimes. As we move toward our priority goals, the foundation for our activities will be the effective use of technology, a global perspective, and strengthening the many partnerships on which we rely.

Regulatory Priorities

To support our goal of effectively administering the Bank Secrecy Act, a key priority is to effectively tailor the regulatory regime for the money services businesses industry. We will continue to enhance our outreach activities to that industry by using information from law enforcement partners that encounter potential unregistered money services businesses to focus our education initiatives, and we are translating our money services business informational brochures into seven different languages.

We will also work with the Internal Revenue Service, the Conference of State Bank Supervisors, and the Money Transmitter Regulators Association to better utilize educational information already available and to develop training materials for use by federal and state money services business examiners. This initiative will promote better consistency across industries.

To further strengthen BSA administration, we plan to:

- Develop a regulatory framework for stored value products/services that reflects ongoing changes in that industry.

- Implement an action plan to address concerns among domestic and international policymakers, law enforcement, and financial institutions about the misuse of various types of business entities (e.g., corporations, limited liability companies, limited partnerships, trusts, etc.) to facilitate money laundering and other financial crimes.

- Publish additional BSA guidance to financial institutions in order to improve consistency in the interpretation and application of BSA regulations.

- Develop reports that detail industry compliance with the Bank Secrecy Act and identify compliance deficiencies to assist in the promulgation of guidance to industries and regulatory examiners.

- Establish an approach for responding to comments on the question of whether to lower the dollar threshold for the requirement to collect, retain, and transmit information transmittals of funds.

Regulatory Priorities (continued...)

To continue to extend BSA regulations to various financial industries listed in the USA PATRIOT Act, we plan to finalize anti-money laundering program rules for investment advisers, commodity trading advisors, and commodity pool operators. We will also continue to research the potential for proposed rulemakings requiring loan or finance companies, including government-sponsored enterprises, to establish anti-money laundering programs.

Bank Secrecy Act Reporting and Information

Pending Departmental and Congressional approval, we will continue to study and plan for a system to collect cross-border wire transfer data. We will also continue to expand access to the BSA data so that authorized law enforcement and regulatory users can quickly and efficiently query that data when needed.

Optimizing the integrity and value of the BSA data remains a key objective. We will continue to implement data quality measures and to examine the overall data collection process. We will also maintain our focus on promoting electronic filing of BSA reports as a way to enhance speed, economy, and data quality. We will continue to provide outreach and technical assistance to expand e-filing by covered institu-

tions, especially the largest report filers. We will also monitor customer satisfaction with e-filing and, if necessary, improve the system to meet filer needs.

To pursue the enhanced customer service envisioned through the BSA Direct Retrieval and Sharing project halted this year, we will begin a re-planning effort to identify needs and any reusable components from the earlier project. We expect the effort to benefit from our new Project Management Office, initiated in Fiscal Year 2006, as well as from stronger processes for governing information technology investment decisions and financial oversight.

Analysis

In the analytic arena, we will continue to enhance the value of our support to law enforcement agencies by focusing on actionable analyses targeted at high-priority money laundering and terrorist financing targets. We will take full advantage of sources of and resources for financial intelligence by completing collaborative analytic efforts with other financial intelligence units, law enforcement agencies, and the intelligence community. We also will continue to collaborate on analytical projects with key federal law enforcement task forces/initiatives, such as the FBI's Terrorist Financing Operations Section, the Drug Enforcement Administration's Fusion

Center, Customs and Border Protection's Tactical Analysis Group, and Immigration and Customs Enforcement's Financial and Trade Division.

Collaborative efforts like these benefit all involved. For example, the Federal Bureau of Investigation recently reviewed SARs coded as indicators of suspected terrorist financing. The FBI found that 20 percent of those SARs contained names of subjects of open FBI terrorism investigations, a very high rate of return.

During the coming year, FinCEN analysts will work jointly with the FBI's Terrorist Financing Operations Section and the Foreign Terrorist Tracking Task Force to exploit information, specifically BSA data and other data sets, encapsulated in the FBI's Investigative Data Warehouse (IDW). Through analysis of these records, we expect to identify policy needs and compliance issues, and to provide valuable feedback to the regulated industries.

A specific goal of this effort will be to identify any commonalities in anti-money laundering programs of institutions that filed these SARs. Where commonalities are found, FinCEN will relay appropriate information back to the financial industry as a way to help other financial institutions improve their anti-money laundering programs.

Another analytical priority is to publish a technical reference guide for law enforcement officials describing money services businesses. The guide will describe traditional types of remittances and services, as well as emerging services such as online payments and prepaid card services.

To improve services to our partners, we will seek to increase the percentage of customers finding FinCEN's analytic reports and publications highly valuable and to continue to increase the amount of complex work done by our analysts. We will also strive to further reduce the time required to transmit SARs stemming from financial institution tips on our Hotline to law enforcement or the intelligence community and the time expended to complete targeted financial institution reviews for our regulatory partners.

International Analysis and Collaboration

Given the vital importance of international cooperation in reducing threats to the security and safety of all nations, we will strengthen our efforts to identify global money laundering and terrorist financing threats in vulnerable geographic areas and industries. Our work will include:

- Collaborating with other members of the Egmont Group of FIUs to improve understanding of how emerging payments methods, such as internet-based payments methods, might be illicitly exploited.

- Working with Egmont Group partners to develop actionable intelligence concerning illicit money flows across the northern and southwestern borders of the United States.

- Developing and implementing an analytic approach to identifying and assessing potential targets for application of Treasury authorities on terrorist financing and money laundering.

- Increasing the pace of our information exchanges with other Egmont Group members.

In addition, we will continue to strengthen FIUs around the globe. In the coming year, we plan to more effectively target our technical assistance and training efforts to FIUs with specific needs. For example, we aim to provide greater and more sustained technical assistance to Egmont Group candidates under our sponsorship, and to Egmont members whose organizational capabilities have been strained by growing needs to collect and analyze financial intelligence and to build the information technology infrastructure for these activities.

We also plan to provide more customized technical assistance and training to meet the needs of specific FIUs in vulnerable geographic areas and areas such as Africa that are currently underrepresented in the Egmont Group. To leverage resources for these efforts, we plan to continue to partner with agencies such as the World Bank, International Monetary Fund, and U.S. Department of State.

In addition, we will continue to deepen and strengthen our ties with strategic Egmont partners as a way to reduce global vulnerability to terrorist financing and other financial crimes. We foresee more collaborative joint analytical projects, personnel exchanges, and streamlined processes for exchanging valuable information in a more timely way.

As an aid to international collaboration, we expect to complete the modernization of the Egmont Secure Web during the next year. The modernization effort includes migrating all accounts and services to a new platform, replacing older equipment and tools, and ensuring high system performance and availability.

Management Priorities

A critical FinCEN management priority for the next year is strengthening our information technology infrastructure. For example, we will expand service continuity capabilities of several critical systems that support both internal and external customers. We will also seek to improve operational efficiency of our internal network, reduce costs, and increase system availability. We expect to expand and establish performance measures for our enterprise architecture, adopt improved technology investment management techniques and controls, and improve data quality.

To pursue our management aim of attracting and developing a high-performing, diverse work force, we plan to:

- Strengthen employee recruitment and hiring by implementing Career Connector, an online recruitment system, as well as increasing use of approved hiring flexibilities.

- Ensure that new and current employees have the skills they need to achieve our mission by assessing competency gaps for mission-critical occupations, designing a training strategy for managers in support of succession planning, and developing new programs for mentoring, professional development, and rotational assignments. In addition, we will develop a comprehensive program to provide basic and advanced training for our financial intelligence analysts.

We will also continue efforts begun in Fiscal Year 2006 to improve our processes for overseeing and managing tasks and projects. For example, we will develop the charter, organizational structure, and operating principles for our new Project Management Office. Further, we will staff the office, train a cadre of internal project managers, adopt proven methodologies, and establish a portfolio of key projects.

Finally, we will enhance both internal and external communications during Fiscal Year 2007. We will update our Strategic Plan, enhance our employee Intranet, and redesign our public website, www.fincen.gov, to improve content, organization, design, navigation, and ease of use.

The Financial Crimes Enforcement Network includes the Office of the Director and four major operating divisions. In addition, the Office of Chief Counsel, which reports to the U.S. Department of the Treasury, provides legal services for FinCEN. Descriptions of these units and biographies of key officials follow:

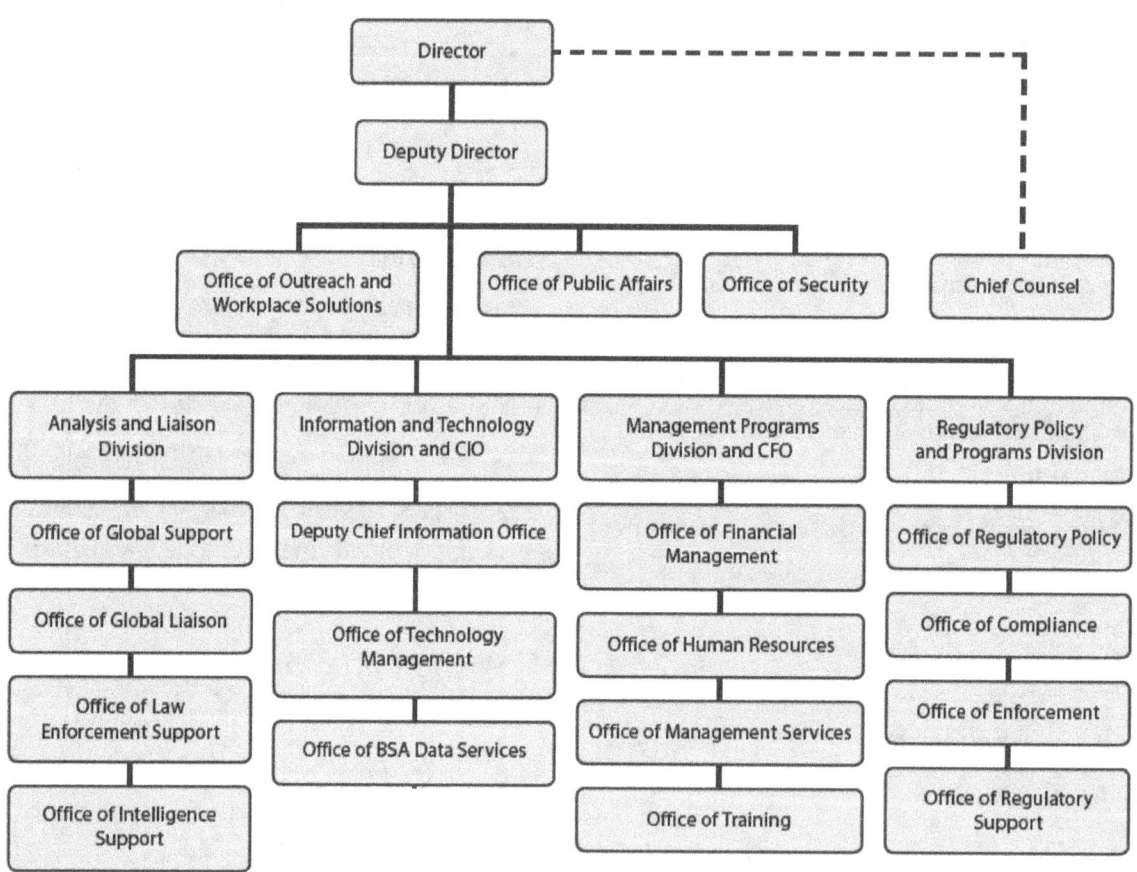

Office of the Director

The Office of the Director is made up of FinCEN's top executives and support staff. William F. Baity, FinCEN's Deputy Director since January 1995, is currently Acting Director. He succeeded Robert W. Werner, who was appointed the fifth Director of FinCEN on March 6, 2006, by the Secretary of the Treasury and served in that role through December 2006. William J. Fox served as Director from December 1, 2003 through February 3, 2006.

The Office of the Director establishes, oversees, and implements policies to detect and prevent money laundering and terrorist financing. In addition to the Director and Deputy Director, this unit includes the Office of Security, Office of Outreach and Workplace Solutions, and Office of Public Affairs.

Office of Chief Counsel

The attorneys and support staff of the Office of the Chief Counsel provide legal advice to FinCEN officials across the full range of their responsibilities, including issues relating to the administration of the Bank Secrecy Act, domestic and international aspects of information law, inter-agency information sharing, the use of information in enforcement operations and proceedings, international law relating to counter-money laundering efforts, and administrative law. The office also provides advice and training on ethics issues.

Cynthia Clark was named Acting Chief Counsel in September 2006. Her predecessor was Brian L. Ferrell.

Office of Chief Counsel Activity, Fiscal Years 2004 – 2006

	FY 2004	FY 2005	FY 2006
Regulations and Federal Register Notices issued	28	6	25
Advisories issued	5	1	4
Memoranda of Understanding completed	28	84	45
Regulatory rulings issued	3	6	3
Enforcement actions	4	3	10

Analysis and Liaison Division

FinCEN is the largest overt collector of financial crimes intelligence in the United States. The information we collect under the Bank Secrecy Act is highly valuable in combating terrorism and investigating money laundering and other financial crime. FinCEN's Analysis and Liaison Division is responsible for:

- Analyzing BSA data and other information to produce analytic products supporting the needs of domestic law enforcement, intelligence, and foreign financial intelligence unit customers, and

- Liaison with domestic law enforcement agencies and with counterpart financial

intelligence units in other countries, and provision of direct, secure access to BSA data for domestic law enforcement and regulatory agencies.

The division's analytic products range in complexity from traditional suspect-related reports to policy-level assessments of financial crimes threats. Consistent with FinCEN's strategic plan, analytic resources are being transitioned toward analysis that focuses increasingly on FinCEN's unique skills and knowledge of BSA data.

Patrick Conlon was appointed FinCEN's Associate Director for Analysis in August 2006. His predecessor was David M. Vogt.

Analytic Products – Fiscal Years 2005 – 2006

	FY 2005	FY 2006
"Complex" analytical products[1]	140	176
"Basic" analytic products[2]	1,298	1,284[3]
Total analytic products completed by FinCEN employees and contractors	1,438	1,460
Number of subjects researched by FinCEN employees and contractors	8,877	7,462[3]

[1] "Complex" products include synthesis of data from multiple sources, interpretation of findings and recommendations for action and/or policy. Examples are geographic threat assessments, analyses of money laundering/illicit financing methodologies, analytic support for major law enforcement investigations, and analysis of Bank Secrecy Act compliance patterns.

[2] "Basic" products consist of suspect-based database queries and reports requiring relatively straightforward interpretation of findings.

[3] Decrease reflects the Financial Crimes Enforcement Network's strategy of increasingly focusing resources on products requiring unique and specialized analysis.

Information and Technology Division and Chief Information Officer

The Information and Technology Division, headed by our Chief Information Officer, is responsible for managing the BSA data store. The division performs a variety of roles related to the collection and processing of BSA data and manages the technical infrastructure supporting FinCEN's day-to-day operations. The Information and Technology Division is comprised of the Office of the Deputy CIO, Office of Technology Management, and Office of BSA Data Services.

Edward J. Dorris was selected as the Chief Information Officer and Associate Director for the Information and Technology Division in September 2006. His predecessor was Jack Cunniff.

Key Facts about Electronic Filing and Use of Bank Secrecy Act Data

	FY 2004	FY 2005	FY 2006
Number of users accessing BSA data electronically	2,181	3,344	4,683
Share of BSA filings submitted electronically last two months of year	20%	29%	48%
Cost per BSA Form E-Filed	0.64	0.32	0.22
Customer satisfaction with BSA Direct E-Filing Component	N/A	N/A	92%
Number of requests for specific sensitive financial information transmitted from federal law enforcement agencies to financial institutions	198	92	125
Number of federal users mining the BSA data downloaded to their agencies	New	1,154	2,457

Management Programs Division and Chief Financial Officer

Headed by our Chief Financial Officer, the Management Programs Division provides financial, planning, performance measurement, human resources, and logistical services critical to the operations of the bureau. This division includes four offices: Financial Management, Management Services, Human Resources, and Training. A Project Management Office will be staffed in Fiscal Year 2007.

Diane K. Wade has served as Associate Director and Chief Financial Officer since November 2004. In this role, she is responsible for assuring the integrity of the fiscal and property accountability and the implementation of sound accounting, reporting, and financial management policies.

Regulatory Policy and Programs Division

Pursuant to FinCEN's authority to administer the Bank Secrecy Act, and in conjunction with the other divisions, FinCEN's Regulatory Policy and Programs Division issues regulations, regulatory rulings, and interpretive guidance; assists state and federal regulatory agencies to more consistently and robustly examine financial institutions for BSA compliance; takes appropriate enforcement action against financial institutions that violate the Bank Secrecy Act; engages in outreach to financial institutions, law enforcement authorities, and regulatory agencies; and provides comprehensive analytical support through sophisticated data mining and complex analysis of BSA filings. These activities span the breadth of the financial services industry, including—but not limited to—banks and other depository institutions, money services businesses, securities broker-dealers, mutual funds, futures commission merchants and introducing brokers in commodities, dealers in precious metals, precious stones, or jewels, insurance companies, and casinos.

Jamal El-Hindi was named Associate Director for Regulatory Policy and Programs in May 2006. His predecessor was William D. Langford. The Division is comprised of the Office of Regulatory Policy, the Office of Compliance, the Office of Enforcement, and the Office of Regulatory Analysis.

Summary of Bank Secrecy Act Form Revisions and Rule Making– Fiscal Year 2006

Bank Secrecy Act forms revised	Suspicious Activity Report by: ■ Casinos and Card Clubs ■ Depository Institutions ■ Securities and Futures Industries ■ Money Services Business
New Bank Secrecy Act form	Suspicious Activity Report by Insurance Companies
Bank Secrecy Act forms renewed without change	Sixty-day and 30-day Federal Register notices were published to renew: ■ Report of International Transportation of Currency and Monetary Instruments (no comments received) ■ Report of Cash Payments Over $10,000 Received in a Trade or Business-Form 8300 (no comments received) ■ Currency Transaction Report-Casinos (no comments received) ■ Currency Transaction Report Casinos-Nevada (no comments received ■ Currency Transaction Report (four respondents provided comments)
New Bank Secrecy Act final rules issued	■ Anti-Money Laundering Programs: Special Due Diligence Programs for Certain Foreign Accounts ■ Requirement that Mutual Funds Report Suspicious Transactions ■ Anti-Money Laundering Programs for Insurance Companies ■ Requirement that Insurance Companies Report Suspicious Transactions.
Bank Secrecy Act rules renewed without change	Sixty-day and 30-day Federal Register notices were published to renew: ■ Anti-Money Laundering program rules for money services businesses; mutual funds; operators of credit card systems; unregistered investment companies; dealers in precious metals, precious stones, or jewels; and insurance companies; and ■ Customer Identification Program rules for futures commission merchants and introducing brokers; banks, savings associations, credit unions, and certain non-federally regulated banks; mutual funds; and broker-dealers

Key Regulatory Data – Fiscal Years 2005 – 2006

	FY 2005	FY 2006
Number of federal, state, and territorial financial regulators with whom information-sharing agreements have been executed	41	48
Number of compliance matters referred to FinCEN for review and, as appropriate, consideration of possible enforcement action	233	268
Number of regulatory inquiries answered	7,612	9,599[1]

[1] Total includes 7,877 Helpline inquiries, 196 Financial Institution Hotline inquiries, 263 Webmaster inquiries, 83 correspondence inquiries, and 1,180 publication requests.

FinCEN is a small, growing bureau. As of September 30, 2006, we had a staff of 299, including 28 managers.

Financial Crimes Enforcement Network Staff

	Fiscal Year 2004	Fiscal Year 2005	Fiscal Year 2006
Employees on board (as of end of fiscal year)	253	291	299
New hires	35	64	50
Departures	27	18	42

Number of On-board Employees by Division

Division	September 30, 2004	September 30, 2005	September 30, 2006
Office of the Director	24	33	26
Office of Chief Counsel	11	11	9
Analytics[1]	82	83	N/A
Analysis and Liaison	N/A	N/A	109
Client Liaison and Services[2]	79	80	N/A
Information Technology	N/A	N/A	40
Management Programs	32	35	39
Regulatory Policy and Programs	25	49	76
Total	253	291	299

[1] The Analytics Division became the Analysis and Liaison Division in FY 2006, and was expanded to include employees formerly in the Client Liaison and Services Division who provide liaison services with law enforcement agencies and other financial intelligence units.

[2] The Client Liaison and Services Division was disbanded in FY 2006. Employees from this Division moved into the new Analysis and Liaison Division or into the new Division of Information Technology.

Managers and Non-supervisory Employees

	September 30, 2004	September 30, 2005	September 30, 2006
Senior Executive Service	4	7	4
Other Managers	22	20	24
Nonsupervisory Employees	227	264	271

Financial Crimes Enforcement Network Diversity Profile, September 30, 2006

	Male	Female	Total
Total employees	44.41%	55.59%	100%
Hispanic/Latino	0.68%	2.03%	2.71%
White	33.90%	36.61%	70.51%
Black/African American	6.78%	13.22%	20%
American Indian/Alaska Native	0%	0.68%	0.68%
Asian	3.05%	3.05%	6.10%
Employees with Disabilities	Not Available	Not Available	4.41%

In Fiscal Year 2006, FinCEN's appropriated budget was nearly $73 million.

History of President's Budget Requests and Appropriations, Fiscal Years 2004 – 2006

(Dollars in thousands)

	FY 2004	FY 2005	FY 2006
President's Budget Request	$57,571	$64,502	$73,630
Final Appropriated Enacted Level	$57,231	$71,922	$72,894

The following Congressional Committees and Subcommittees have authorizing and appropriations responsibilities for our operations.

U.S. House of Representatives Committees

- Committee on Financial Services, Subcommittee on Oversight and Investigations (Authorizing Committee)

- Committee on Appropriations, Subcommittee on Transportation, Treasury, Housing and Urban Development, the Judiciary, and the District of Columbia (Appropriating Committee)

U.S. Senate Committees

- Committee on Banking, Housing, and Urban Affairs (Authorizing Committee)

- Committee on Appropriations, Subcommittee on Transportation, Treasury, the Judiciary, Housing and Urban Development, and Related Agencies (Appropriating Committee)

Farewell from Former Director to FinCEN Employees

"I would like to thank each and every one of you from the bottom of my heart for your support and dedicated professionalism shown to me and the Financial Crimes Enforcement Network during my 2+ year tenure at the agency. Always remember that this agency has a mission that is critical to the economic and national security of our country and that your work in achieving this mission makes a real difference for our country. I leave with full confidence that you will carry on and succeed, and I wish you all the very best—both personally and professionally—as you continue on."

William J. Fox, former Director, Financial Crimes Enforcement Network
Upon his resignation, February 3, 2006

FinCEN works closely with regulatory, law enforcement, private sector, and international partners. Organizations with which we have strong working relationships include the Bank Secrecy Act Advisory Group, the federal supervisory agencies, and the Egmont Group, all described below.

Bank Secrecy Act Advisory Group

Congress established the Bank Secrecy Act Advisory Group in 1992 to enable the financial services industry and law enforcement to advise the Secretary of the Treasury on ways to enhance the utility of BSA records and reports. Since 1994, the Advisory Group has served as a forum for industry, regulators, and law enforcement to communicate about how SARs and other BSA reports are used by law enforcement and how record keeping and reporting requirements can be improved. The Director of FinCEN chairs the Bank Secrecy Act Advisory Group.

The Bank Secrecy Act Advisory Group, which is not subject to the Federal Advisory Committee Act, meets twice each year in Washington, D.C.

Since the enactment of the USA PATRIOT Act of 2001, which expanded BSA requirements to new industries, FinCEN has been taking steps to ensure that the Bank Secrecy Act Advisory Group continues to fully and fairly reflect the entire BSA constituency. The Advisory Group now has 50 members.

The Bank Secrecy Act Advisory Group utilizes a variety of permanent and ad hoc subcommittees to identify and analyze relevant issues. Current subcommittees focus on: suspicious activity reporting issues; BSA examination consistency; wire transfer reporting thresholds; privacy/security issues; non-bank financial institutions issues; securities/futures issues; law enforcement issues; and currency transaction reporting issues. The Bank Secrecy Act Advisory Group also co-chairs publication of *The SAR Activity Review—Trends, Tips & Issues*, which provides meaningful information to the financial community about the preparation, use, and value of SARs.

Need for Partnership between Government and Financial Institutions

... the success of this [Bank Secrecy Act] regime depends upon the government and financial institutions acting in true partnership – each committed to the goal of taking reasonable steps to ensure that the financial system is protected from criminals and terrorists to the greatest extent possible through the development of appropriate programs and the sharing and dissemination of information.

Robert W. Werner,
Director, Financial Crimes Enforcement Network
Before the Senate Banking Committee
September 12, 2006

Federal Regulatory Agencies

Responsibility for conducting BSA compliance examinations has been delegated to the following federal agencies:

- Federal Deposit Insurance Corporation

- Board of Governors of the Federal Reserve System

- Office of the Comptroller of the Currency (U.S. Department of the Treasury)

- Internal Revenue Service, Small Business/ Self-Employed Division (U.S. Department of the Treasury)

- Office of Thrift Supervision (U.S. Department of the Treasury)

- National Credit Union Administration

- U.S. Securities and Exchange Commission

- Commodity Futures Trading Commission

FinCEN assists and supports these agencies to promote effective and uniform application of the BSA regulations.

The Egmont Group

The Egmont Group is a global association of financial intelligence units (FIUs), national centers that have been set up to collect information on suspicious or unusual financial activity from the financial industry and designated non-financial businesses and professions, to analyze the data, and to make it available to appropriate national authorities and other FIUs for use in combating terrorist funding and other financial crime. The Group takes its name from the palace in Brussels where 15 financial intelligence units first met in 1995 to establish an informal group for sharing information about money laundering. In Fiscal Year 2006, the Group had 101 members.

FinCEN has played a major role in promoting the multilateral work of the Egmont Group by helping other countries develop their FIUs and assisting already-established units to strengthen anti-terrorist financing and money laundering policies and programs. We also sponsor new FIUs for membership in the group and provide and maintain a secure web system through which Egmont members can exchange information.

Our Deputy Director chairs the Egmont Committee, which coordinates Egmont Group activities. We also provide staff support for Egmont's five Working Groups, which are described below:

- The Outreach Working Group seeks to create a global network of financial intelligence units by identifying candidates for membership and FIU sponsors to work with them to ensure that they meet international standards.

- The Legal Working Group reviews the candidacy of potential members and handles all legal aspects and matters of principle within Egmont, including

cooperation between FIUs.

- The Training Working Group identifies, plans, coordinates, and implements training opportunities for financial intelligence unit personnel. The Training Working Group has also published a collection of sanitized terrorist financing and money laundering cases that were used at the typology exercises of the Financial Action Task Force, an intergovernmental body that develops and promotes national and international policies to combat money laundering and terrorist financing, as well as by the World Bank and the United Nations Office of Drug Control for training purposes.

- The Operational Working Group seeks to bring FIUs together to collaborate on cases and strategic projects such as insurance schemes and stored value.

- The Information Technology Working Group examines new software applications that might facilitate analytical work and focuses on such issues as data mining, information fusion, and security.

The following publications, all produced in Fiscal Year 2006, are available on the Financial Crimes Enforcement Network's website, www.fincen.gov.

- *Financial Crimes Enforcement Network Annual Report for Fiscal Year 2005*

- *SAR Activity Review – Trends, Tips and Issues* – Issue 9, October 2005

- *SAR Activity Review – Trends, Tips and Issues* – Issue 10, May 2006

- *SAR Activity Review – By the Numbers* – Issue 5, February 2006

- *SAR Activity Review – By the Numbers* – Issue 6, May 2006

Earlier issues of the publications above are also available on our website.

The Reference Series: Postal Money Orders published in Fiscal Year 2006 is an Official Use Only document available to law enforcement, intelligence, and regulatory agencies. For further information about this manual, e-mail webmaster@fincen.gov, call (703) 905-3591, or write to us:

Financial Crimes Enforcement Network
Post Office Box 39
Vienna, VA 22183-0039.

FinCEN relies on internal and external evaluations to gauge program effectiveness and make improvements as needed. Listed below are key evaluations completed and underway during Fiscal Year 2006.

Program Assessment Rating Tool

The Program Assessment Rating Tool (PART) is a systematic method of assessing the performance of program activities across the federal government. It is composed of a series of questions designed to assess program performance related to the Government Performance and Results Act and the goals of the President's Management Agenda. Answers to PART questions must be supported by objective data.

In Fiscal Year 2006, two FinCEN programs underwent PART evaluation. First, an evaluation of the Bank Secrecy Act Analysis program found that FinCEN has developed plans to expand the percentage of advanced analytical products produced, but significant effort will be required to achieve its long-term targets. Also, FinCEN will work to measure the impact of its efforts to strengthen anti-terrorist financing and anti-money laundering programs worldwide. Second, an evaluation of the BSA Administration found that FinCEN had made progress in executing memoranda of understanding agreements governing the exchange of information with federal and state regulatory agencies. However, additional time is needed to ensure BSA compliance in more vulnerable industries. FinCEN will work to address the PART recommendations and better measure the outcomes of its programs.

Customer Surveys

FinCEN contracted with external organizations to conduct three independent customer surveys in areas related to our performance measures. These surveys covered customers of our regulatory resource center, recipients of our analytic support, and filers who use the BSA e-Filing system.

Government Accountability Office Audits

Completed in FY 2006:

- GAO-06-386: Opportunities Exist for FinCEN and the Banking Regulators to Further Strengthen the Framework for Consistent BSA Oversight

- GAO-06-483: International Financial Crime: Treasury's Roles and Responsibilities Relating to Selected Provisions of the USA PATRIOT Act, June 2006

- GAO-06-947R: Observations on the Financial Crimes Enforcement Network's BSA Direct Retrieval and Sharing Project, July 2006

Underway in FY 2006:

- Joint Review of FinCEN's and IRS' Management of the Bank Secrecy Act

Treasury Office of Inspector General Audits

Completed in FY 2006:

- OIG-06-030: FinCEN Has Taken Steps to Better Analyze Bank Secrecy Act Data But Challenges Remain, May 2006

Underway in FY 2006:

- Treasury's Administration of the Bank Secrecy Act

Internal Assessments

Completed in FY 2006:

- Internal control review of laptop accountability

- Internal control review of travel card program

- Internal control review of blanket purchase agreements

Treasury Financial Management Assessment

Using criteria from the Office of Management and Budget, the Treasury Department sets standards for "green," "yellow," and "red" performance in financial management and regularly monitors key performance indicators. The table that follows shows our Fiscal Year 2006 record in meeting the standards for "green" performance.

Financial Area	Treasury Standard for "Green"	FinCEN FY 2006 Average	FinCEN Score
Percent of cash reconciled to total	>99.99%	100%	Green
Percent of uncleared suspense transactions over 60 days	<10%	0%	Green
Percent of accounts receivable from public delinquent over180 days	<10%	21%*	Red
Percent of electronic vendor payments	96%	100%	Green
Percent non-credit card invoices paid on time	>98%	99.75%	Green
Percent of centrally billed travel cards with balances over 61 days past due	0%	0%	Green
Percent of individually billed travel cards with balances over 61 days past due	<2%	1%	Green
Percent of purchase cards with balances over 61 days past due	0%	0%	Green

*This percentage reflects overdue accounts receivable currently in litigation.

The following material supplements the discussion of program evaluations beginning on page 63:

Key Performance Measures

Measure	FY 2005	FY 2006	FY 2007 Target
Number of federal and state regulatory agencies with which FinCEN has concluded memoranda of understanding/ information sharing agreements	41	48	50
Percentage of Regulatory Resource Center customers rating the guidance received as understandable	New	94%	90%
Average time to process enforcement matters	1.3 years	1 year	1 year
Percentage of bank examinations conducted by the Federal Banking Agencies indicating a systemic failure of the anti-money laundering program rule	7.9%	8.0%	Baseline
Percentage of customers finding FinCEN's analytic reports highly valuable	New	77%	78%
Percentage of customers satisfied with the BSA Direct E-Filing component	New	92%	90%

In addition, one of FinCEN's management priorities is to develop a performance measure for the impact of program activities on preventing the misuse of the financial system by those engaged in illicit activities.

Finally, as a clarification, the Office of Management and Budget does not review or assess the Treasury Department financial performance assessment described on pages 64-65 of the report.